PRAISE GOD ...
I'M SICK!

encouragement for those facing illness

Raymond C. Hundley Ph. D.
B.A., M.A.R., M. Litt., Ph.D.

Christian Apologetics Publications
Sarasota, Florida

ISBN: 1494224186
ISBN 13: 9781494224189
Library of Congress Control Number: 2015904930
CreateSpace Independent Publishing Platform
North Charleston, South Carolina

All Scripture quotations, unless otherwise indicated, are taken from the New American Standard Bible®, copyright 1960, 1962, 1963, 1968, 1971, 1972, 1973, 1975, 1977, 1995 by the Lockman Foundation, The Zondervan NASB Study Bible, 1999. Used by permission.

Christian Apologetics Publications
926 Ell Way
Sarasota, Florida 34243

DEDICATION

I want to dedicate this book to the
memory of "Mema" (Mrs. Undine C. White),
my mother-in-law, who showed
us how to suffer through illness with a
sweet, loving, unselfish spirit that
blessed everyone who visited her.
The afternoon of her passing into heaven
was one of the most beautiful and
meaningful experiences our extended
family has ever had.

TABLE OF CONTENTS

INTRODUCTION

Don't get me wrong - I fully believe in divine healing. I have prayed for many people and many of them have been miraculously healed by the Lord. I have been healed. My family has been healed. We believe in healing, but we just don't believe it is always guaranteed, instantaneous, and predictable. The question I want to explore in this book is: *what do you do when you're between healings?* That is, what do you do when you've prayed for healing and others have prayed for your healing, but you're still sick? Is there no word from the Lord for those of us who live in sickness and suffering? What can we say as Christians to those who live year after year with life-limiting disabilities? Surely there is a word from the Lord for those 650 million disabled people who make up 10% of the world's population!

I have been ill for the past several years. I have struggled with diabetes, arthritis, congestive heart failure, iron deficiency anemia, neuropathy, low kidney function, and chronic fatigue. It has not been easy sometimes to deal with all of this. Part of the struggle has been the pain of giving up the things I used to find so fulfilling that I can't do any more. I had to take early retirement from my college teaching on World Religions, which I loved, and which touched the lives of thousands of college students with the Gospel. I have had to go on disability and have not been able to work anymore (except writing!). At times, I have been so weak I could hardly stand up or walk. It hurts me to watch my wife having to do work that I used to do, but no longer can.

I have been prayed over by my pastors, our entire Sunday School class, most of the members of our church, a visiting evangelist known for healing, my children and grandchildren, believers in Kenya (thanks to my missionary sister), the famous healer from the Lakeland Revival, a missionary to Mexico who has healed many people, and I have prayed for my own healing, begging the Lord to restore me so

I could serve Him more effectively. I have prayed in faith. There is no unconfessed sin in my life. I firmly believe that the Lord can heal me, *but He hasn't done it ... yet.* So, what do I do now?

Are those of us who aren't healed some kind of "spiritual lepers" that have to be kept in the shadows so that the unbelievers won't see that sometimes Christianity doesn't "work"? I don't believe that for a minute. In fact, I believe that God can use us to witness to the world with amazing power and victory, even in (and through) our suffering.

A brief perusal of *Amazon.com* under the heading "Healing" yields over 52,000 results! Titles include: *Healing, Bible Healing Study Course, Healing Belongs to Us, Healing Is a Choice, The Secret of Instant Healing, If You Need Healing Do These Things, How to Receive and Keep Your Healing, The Prayer That Heals, Healing Forever Settled, Healing - It Is Always God's Will, The Power to Heal,* and many others. Authors like Francis MacNutt, Kenneth Copeland, John Wember, T. L. Osborn, Oral Roberts, Kenneth Hagin, and Robert Tilton are eager to explain how to be healed and how to heal others through God's incredible power. A seemingly never-ending parade of personal testimonies give ample evidence of miraculous healings of everything from cancer to heart attacks to A.I.D.S. to toothaches. There are even CDs for sale in which "anointed healers" read healing Scriptures and pray for your healing.

It is almost overwhelming. Given all these resources, it's a wonder any committed Christian is ever sick for more than two seconds! The Prosperity Gospel/Word of Faith movement has summarized the case for guaranteed healing in seven easy steps, which I call the *"Prosperity Package"*:

1. All sickness is an oppression from Satan.
2. God wants us to be healthy all the time and He fights against Satan.
3. God is more powerful than Satan.
4. The healing of all illness was assured through Jesus' atonement on the cross ("by His stripes we are healed").

5. If we have enough faith, God will always heals us.
6. If we aren't healed, it's either because we don't have enough faith, or there is sin in our lives, or we *are* healed, but it hasn't been *manifested* yet.
7. God has a set time for each person to die and He brings the person to Himself when that time comes.

The Prosperity Package is easy to understand and apply. The problem is, it doesn't always work and it is not biblically sound. As we will see in this book, there is a great deal of biblical teaching about sickness, suffering, and afflictions that contradicts the "Prosperity Package" at almost every point. Besides, it doesn't work. There are millions of sincere, faith-filled Christians in the world today who suffer daily from diseases that are not healed, even though they ask the Lord to heal them. And when the "Prosperity Package" doesn't produce the promised results, the "anointed healers" sometimes turn on the victims, accusing them and creating a situation of despair, self-doubt, and depression that can even be life-threatening.

A couple that my wife and I led to the Lord many years ago entered the ministry and began pastoring a church. The husband soon became very ill with cancer and went to their support group for prayer. A "prophet" in the group gave a "word of knowledge from the Lord" saying that he would be on his deathbed, but the Lord would raise him up to health again. Well, he was soon on his deathbed, but the Lord did not raise him up - he died. A few days after the funeral, some members of the prayer group visited the young widow and told her that if she had exercised enough faith, her husband would still be alive. She almost lost her mind. She called us in such turmoil that we were afraid she might commit suicide. We talked to her on the phone and I even wrote an answer to the attack by those deluded people, and she finally came around. She fought back to a position of faith again, but it was nip-and-tuck there for a while. Many people find themselves in this same heart-rending struggle. Some have even left the faith because of it.

Recently as I entered my church's sanctuary a man I don't know walked up next to me and said, "Do you think your sickness is an attack from Satan?" I answered quickly, "No, I don't." Before I could give any details about my answer, he forcefully said, "Well, I do!" And then he walked away. I was shocked that someone would say that kind of thing to me and just walk away. But it convinced me even more of the need for a book like this one.

So what do I do if I've prayed and prayed, and others have prayed for me, but I am still sick? Do I walk away in shame and disillusionment and just give up? Do I doubt God's love for me, or His ability to heal me, or His willingness to heal me? Do I claim that I actually *am healed*, but it just hasn't been *manifested* yet? Do I run from healer to healer, believing that if I just find the right one, God will do it? Do I quit encouraging others to pray for healing? Do I just "endure" my illness as I heard a radio preacher suggest? Do I long for death as "the ultimate healing"?

No, I refuse to do any of those things. With God as my witness, I will live through this with victory and hope and faith, and I will find a way to bring glory to God through all of it! This book is an account of how I (and many other people) have tried to do that, *in the meantime*. My prayer is that if you or someone you know is living in the "in-between time," this book will encourage your heart and challenge you with a God-given mission to turn your time of illness and suffering into a time of blessing, praise, and effective witness to others so that you can declare with me, "Praise God, I'm sick!"

1

I'M IN GREAT COMPANY!

I guess it's true that, "Misery loves company!" But that's not a very noble thought. Nevertheless, as a Christian, it's always comforting to know that you are in great company with fellow believers. I am sick, and I am sometimes really "sick of being sick!" But I'm not the only person who has been here. Millions of Christians around the world live through the daily experience of being sick and not being healed. Millions of disabled people live on in spite of their challenges. Even some very famous believers have suffered with sickness. Although the Bible focuses its attention on miraculous healings, not prolonged illnesses, there are still some encouraging biblical examples of people who endured sickness and triumphed over it (see the example of Job in chapter two).

DAVID
In Psalm 6, King David laments his miserable condition and asks God to heal him. He makes it clear that his suffering has been going on for a long time, with no relief. He complains that he is "pining away;" his "bones are dismayed;" he is "weary with sighing;" and he floods his bed with tears every night. Now that is sickness!

In other psalms David says that his strength has dried up. His heart is like wax. His tongue sticks to his palate. He can count all his bones (Psalm 22). He even goes so far as to complain that his bones are on fire; his heart has withered; he has lost his appetite; he groans loudly; and he can't sleep (Psalm 102). David was one sick man! He knew what it was to face sickness and pain day after day with no let-up. In spite of his deep faith in the Lord and his service to God, he went through some very difficult circumstances and cried out to God to deliver him. His bouts with sickness and suffering brought him to despair, but he still trusted in God. He is my brother in suffering! Somehow it's comforting to know that someone like David went through what I face, day after day.

EPAPHRODITUS, TROPHIMUS, AND TIMOTHY
My "great company" also includes several New Testament characters as well. Paul tells the Philippian Christians about Epaphroditus, who "was sick to the point of death" (Philippians 2:27). Paul reports that he "left [Trophimus] sick at Miletus" (2 Timothy 4:20). Rather than healing Trophimus, Paul had to leave him behind. He also tells his young disciple, Timothy, "Use a little wine for the sake of your stomach and your frequent ailments" (1 Timothy 5:23). This example is especially revealing. If Paul could instantaneously heal people at will, why didn't he just insist that God heal Timothy (or Trophimus!)? Why would he suggest the use of wine for Timothy's repeated stomach problems rather than just heal him of them? If it is a question of faith, what modern faith healer could possibly match Paul's level of faith? He healed many people, but not Timothy or Trophimus. So Epaphroditus, Trophimus, and Timothy are in the club with me, and it feels good having them beside me!

PAUL
Paul himself is the foremost member of the club. He suffered from a "thorn in the flesh" that made his ministry very difficult. Indications are that he probably endured the misery of an eye disease that not only made it hard for him to see, but made it hard for people to look at him as well because of his repulsive appearance (see Galatians 4:13-15, 6:11;

and 1 Corinthians 16:21). Paul shares that he prayed three times for God to take the thorn away, but God said no, because "my grace is sufficient for you, for [My] power is perfected in weakness" (2 Corinthians 12:9). Paul went through his sickness with victory, praise, and faith because his sickness had taught him that "when I am weak, then I am strong" (2 Corinthians 12:10). He also believed that his sickness was allowed by God to keep him humble and to show everyone that the power of his ministry was in God, not in himself (2 Corinthians 12:7-9).

Paul is the foremost member of the "Praise God, I'm Sick" Club, and his experience challenges all of us to go through our times of suffering with triumph and trust. We can be victorious even in times of sickness if we trust the Lord that in our weakness, His great power is made perfect. Others will see us struggle and see that we are still joyous and we are used by the Lord, and they will give Him the honor and praise for how He overrides our weaknesses with His great strength and power. Paul is a welcome member in the club - he challenges all of us who suffer from illnesses to rise higher in our reaction to what we suffer and let God show His great power through our physical weakness!

THE HEBREWS 11 GANG

The story of a group of believers who suffered without being delivered is tucked away in the famous faith chapter - Hebrews 11. How many sermons have you heard based on Hebrews 11:1-35a? "By faith, by faith, by faith" - it lists all the great things those champions of the faith were able to do because they believed God. But have you ever heard a sermon based on Hebrews 11:35b-38? That paragraph tells of a group of believers who had faith too, but they did not see miraculous answers to their prayers or get amazing results because of their faith. The passage says that they were tortured, but not released, and died. They experienced mocking, scourging, chains, imprisonment, stoning, and even being sawn in two. They were killed with swords, and they were not delivered, even though they had faith. They were forced to go around dressed only in animal skins, destitute and afflicted. They were treated very badly. They had to hide in deserts, mountains, caves, and holes in the ground, and they were not rescued. But the author of Hebrews says that they were great people - the world was not worthy of them; they "gained approval through their faith" (Hebrews 11:39). Whose approval? *God's approval!*

They had tremendous faith and had God's approval of their faith, but they weren't rescued, they weren't delivered, they suffered without relief, and in many cases, the text says that they died. Doesn't exactly sound like the "Health and Wealth Gospel" we are bombarded with from every side, does it? They are part of the club - an honored part. This world was not worthy of them and the faith that they exercised, but that didn't guarantee that everything would go well for them. They suffered - some of them suffered terribly - but they still maintained their faith in God and He approved of it! What a testimony of the "in-spite-of" kind of faith that can take us through the hard times with victory and a powerful witness to the power of God in our lives!

That's the kind of Christian I want to be. Of course, I would always prefer the "hallelujah" road in which when I believe, God delivers me; but that doesn't always happen. In fact, I'd have to say that it seldom happens that way for me. I *do* have faith, but it is faith in God's trustworthiness and His wisdom and His will, not in some magical formula for getting what I want out of Him. And I am proud to be in the great company of those saints in the latter part of Hebrews 11 who had faith even when things didn't work out for their comfort or even their survival.

AMY CARMICHAEL

Modern examples of this principle abound. Amy Carmichael, the incredible missionary to India's temple child prostitutes, spent the last twenty years of her life crippled due to a fall, unable to walk, in bed, praying for the work she could no longer do, and seeing God bless it even more than when she was young and vibrant. Amy's many books, most of them written during this period of suffering, have been used by the Lord to bless millions of Christians around the world, and her legacy to save children continues today.

CHARLES COWMAN

The famous devotional book, *Streams in the Desert*, was born out of the experience of Charles Cowman, dynamic missionary to the Orient with the Oriental Missionary Society (today called One Mission Society), who spent the last seven years of his life in bed praying for the amazing work God had used him to begin. To minister to him and others in his situation, his wife, Lettie Cowman, collected the anointed writings that were to become that world-renowned devotional classic, *Streams in the Desert*. That book has been mightily used by God to encourage many Christians going through the pain of sickness. Charles Cowman's prayers and his stalwart, Spirit-filled example circled the globe and inspired hundreds of young men and women to enter missionary service (including me).

JONI EARECKSON TADA

Probably the most famous present-day member of the club is Joni Eareckson Tada. Joni jumped into a lake in 1967, fractured her spinal column, and became paralyzed from the neck down. At first, she was angry with God and wanted to kill herself, but a Christian friend led her to a deeper faith in Christ. She writes, "Now I believe that God's purpose in my accident was to turn a stubborn kid into a woman who would reflect patience, endurance and a lively, optimistic hope of the heavenly glories above... I have discovered many good things that have come from my disability. I used to think happiness was a Friday night date, a size 12 dress, and a future with Ethan Allen furniture and 2.5 children. Now I know better. What matters is love." (from "A Victory through Suffering" by Joni Eareckson Tada).

Joni has written many books, shared in conferences all over the world, appeared on TV many times - even four times on *Larry King Live* - and her life story has been made into a movie (*Joni*). Her amazing ability to paint holding a brush in her teeth has inspired many disabled people to do what they can do with what they have. She has led a multifaceted ministry called "Joni and Friends" that produces and distributes books and videos on living with disabilities; raises funds for sharing wheel chairs and the Gospel with disabled people around the world; sponsors family retreats on dealing with disabilities; coordinates Joni's speaking schedule in conferences and interviews; develops materials for disability ministries in local churches; and manages the *Christian Institute on Disability*. She has used her disability and her "in-spite-of" faith in God to bring great glory to the Lord.

On June 24, 2010, Joni announced through her website that she had been diagnosed with breast cancer and would soon be undergoing surgery and chemotherapy. Her declaration of incredible faith in God in spite of this newest suffering is worth quoting:

> … you have heard me often say that our afflictions come from the hand of an all-wise and sovereign God, and although cancer is something new, I want to assure you that I'm genuinely content to receive from God whatever He deems fit for me - even if it is from His left hand … For years I have hoped that my quadriplegia *might* encourage people struggling with cancer … now I have a chance to *truly* empathize and journey alongside, affirming that God's grace is *always* sufficient for whatever the disease or disability … So, there you have it. Breast cancer. But I say it without fear and trembling. I say it with confidence, knowing that God only does things for my good … things which will further His kingdom … things which will cause us to lean even harder on Him. (*joniandfriends.org* - June 24, 2010, #7344)

Joni is a startling, crystal clear example of the basic truths I want to communicate in this book: (1) God does not always heal us. (2) We can trust Him even when we don't understand why He allows something to happen to us or why He doesn't heal us. (3) God can use our suffering for powerful witness to a world waiting to see how Christians can suffer and still have joy and hope. And (4) our sufferings can bring us closer to God if we trust in Him and His goodness and believe He will use us and our suffering to advance His kingdom and bring glory to His Name.

So, I am in *Great Company!* I could go on and on, but suffice it to say that many precious saints have gone through the fire of suffering and sickness and have brought great praise and glory to the Lord by the way they went through it. I have often said that the unbelieving world will seldom listen to the witness of someone for whom everything is easy and suffering-free. But they will stand up and take notice when they see people who can go through suffering with joy in their hearts and praise for God on their lips. I believe that the world is watching to see Christians who can go through the tough times, not be delivered, but still believe in God and show their trust in Him by their joyous, victorious lives. That's a *Great Company* to be in!

2

JOB, IT'S A TRUST ISSUE

T he book of Job has to be one of the most intriguing books in all of the Bible. The drama is intense and the theme is shocking. *Why does a good man have to suffer?* That perennial question still attracts the attention of millions today. Rabbi Harold Kushner's book, *When Bad Things Happen to Good People,* is now almost thirty years old, but it still resonates with thousands and thousands of readers. As the Amazon.com Review states, "This book cannot go unread by anyone who has ever been troubled by the question, 'Why me?'" And who hasn't asked that question? To be human is to ask that question. We all go through "undeserved suffering" and wonder why.

THEODICY

An entire area of theological inquiry - *Theodicy* - is dedicated to that one dilemma. If God is good and all-powerful, why is there evil and suffering in the world? That is the central question of the study of Theodicy. In light of the obvious proliferation of evil and suffering in the world, some theologians have answered that either God is not good, or He is not all-powerful. But neither of those assertions is true. Why does God allow suffering to take place in His world - especially in the lives of good people?

GOD AND SATAN'S FIRST DIALOGUE ABOUT JOB

Again, the book of Job confronts this conundrum and deals with it head-on. It opens with the testimony that Job was indeed a very good man: he "was blameless, upright, fearing God and turning away from evil." What more could you want? This is a very good man. He deserves a standing ovation, not suffering! God should shower him with His best blessings and hold him in the palm of His hand. But Satan, "the adversary," appears on the scene and everything turns sour. When God points to Job as a fine example of a man who fears and obeys Him, Satan says, in essence, "Sure, he obeys You because You protect him and bless him. Withhold Your blessings from him and he will curse You to Your face." You see, Satan is saying that Job doesn't really trust God, he just fawns on God to get what he wants out of Him. Satan insists that if God ever quits being his "blessing-dispenser-machine," Job will turn on Him in an instant. So God allows Satan to test Job to see if what He has said about him is true, but He forbids him to touch him directly.

JOB'S RESPONSE TO HIS SUFFERING

In rapid succession, Job receives messengers who inform him that his sheep and servants have been killed by fire from heaven, his camels and the servants tending them have all fallen under the sword, and a strong wind has demolished the house his sons and daughters were feasting in and they were all killed. Job's response? "The Lord gave and the Lord has taken away. Blessed be the name of the Lord" (Job 1:21). And the text adds, "Through all this Job did not sin nor did he blame [ascribe unseemliness to] God" (Job 1:22). Job has passed the test and still trusts and blesses the Lord in spite of his suffering.

SATAN'S SECOND DIALOGUE WITH GOD

So Satan appears before God again (Job 2:1-6). God points out that Job "still holds fast his integrity, although you incited me to ruin him without cause." Satan sneers that yes, Job has done well, but that if

God touches his "bone and his flesh," he will turn on God and curse Him. So God allows Satan to afflict him, but forbids him to kill him (Job 2:3-6).

JOB'S PERSONAL SUFFERING
Satan afflicts Job with boils from "the sole of his foot to the crown of his head" (2:7). Job's wife responds to this latest attack by counseling him, "Do you still hold fast your integrity? Curse God and die!" (2:9). Job answers his unhelpful wife, "Shall we indeed accept good from God and not accept adversity?" The text adds, "In all this Job did not sin with his lips" (2:10).

It's always interesting that we ask the why question when something bad happens, but we seldom ask why when something good happens. Do we sometimes think we're so good that nothing bad should ever touch us? If we do, we have a distorted view of God, our relationship with Him, and our own lives. Job's trust in God, submission to His will, and acceptance of what God sends his way is incredibly admirable. We would do well to remember it when we suffer relatively minor setbacks compared to the tragedies he endured in his life.

JOB'S "FRIENDS" ATTACK HIM
But Job is not through with his suffering yet. Added to his grief over his children, his loss of livelihood, the attacks of his wife, and his agonizing physical pain, Job is subjected to the visits of three "friends" who come to counsel him in his affliction. Theirs is perhaps the "unkindest cut of all" because they seem set on convincing Job that his suffering is all his own fault. They suggest that it is the result of Job's sin, and that his only way of escape is repentance and full confession. This is echoed today by some who tell those of us who are sick, "It's probably because of unconfessed sin in your life." If there is sin, it is vitally important to repent and confess it, but what if there is no unconfessed sin in your life, as in Job's case? Then you are faced with the impossible task of convincing your "friends" of your

blamelessness before God and challenging their views on who God is and how He deals with human beings.

It is so easy for some people to hold this mechanistic view of God in which if you believe, He heals, unless you have sin in your life. Period. No loose ends. No questions. Just, that's the way it is. But that's *not* the way it is. God doesn't always heal if you have faith, and not being healed does not always indicate that you have unconfessed sin in your life. Job is a perfect example of that truth.

It is so important as you read about Job to remember that God Himself declared him to be blameless, upright, fearing God, and turning away from evil. He is a *good* man, but he suffers. Job's false counselors are wrong. They are wrong about Job and they are wrong about God. Suffering is *not* always punishment. Sometimes it is testing or refining or perfecting or even defeating Satan. God uses suffering in our lives in many ways. Often, our suffering is merely the result of living in a fallen world. It is not automatically a sign of unconfessed sin or lack of faith.

One of the counselors (Job's "friends") says, "Who ever perished being innocent? Or where were the upright destroyed?" (4:7) And the questions rises in me, "Where have you been?" Have you never seen a good person suffer and die? How foolish! It happens all the time. Under what rock was that counselor living?

JESUS OPPOSED THE SAME FALSE BELIEF

Apparently in Jesus' day, this wrong belief was still popular, so He had to answer this falsehood in Luke 13. Commenting about a report of a group of Galileans who had been killed by Pilate as they were sacrificing in the temple, Jesus said, "Do you suppose that these Galileans were greater sinners than all other Galileans because they suffered this fate? I tell you, no ..." (Luke 13:1-3). Again, in the Gospel of John, Jesus' disciples asked Him if a man they saw who was born blind suffered from that disability because he sinned or because his parents sinned. Jesus answered, "It was neither that this man sinned, nor his parents, but it was so that the works of God might be displayed in him" (John 9:1-7). And then Jesus healed him. Suffering is not always the result of sin.

One of Job's other counselors attacks the issue from the opposite side saying, "If you are pure and upright, surely now He would rouse Himself for you and restore your righteous estate." (8:6) In other words, Job if you were really right with God, He would heal you and restore everything you have lost. So, obviously, you are *not* right with God. Again, it is the same indictment of Job and the same incorrect view of God. They insist that righteousness automatically produces blessings, and unrighteousness inevitably produces sufferings. A neat little package, but it is not *true*. Many very righteous people, both in Scripture and today, have suffered terribly; and many unrighteous people have had a great free ride. It is not as simple as the false counselor wants to paint it. And his spiritual descendants abound with us today!

JOB ANSWERS HIS ACCUSERS

Without detailing all the cycles of claims and counterclaims as Job fights off his accusers, we can say that Job goes through periods of deep depression during those debates in which he wishes he had never been born or that he would die. But interspersed with his expressions of depression, we find Job's insistence on the goodness of God. He declares, "You have granted me life and lovingkindness; and Your care has preserved my spirit" (10:12). Job cries out, "Though He slay me, I will hope in Him" (13:15). He testifies, "I know that My Redeemer lives, and at the last He will take His stand on the earth. Even after my skin is destroyed, yet from my flesh I shall see God" (19:25-26). Job is an excellent example of what I have heard my wife, Sharyn, say many times, "Sometimes, all you have left is God, and you find out that He is more than enough." I love her for all the times she has reminded me of that and brought me back to my senses.

GOD RESPONDS TO JOB AND HIS "FRIENDS"

Finally, God answers Job and his counselors. This is what all of us who have read the book have been waiting to hear! Finally, we think, God will set everyone straight and explain why good people suffer and why He doesn't either prevent it or heal it right away. But that doesn't happen. God basically says to Job, "Who do you think you are?" He asks Job a series of questions about creation and nature and His power, asking Job if he can do any of the things that only He can do. Of course, the answer is "no" (38:1-40:1). God's final question to Job levels him, "Will the faultfinder contend with the Almighty? Let him who reproves God answer it" (40:1). Whew, what a question! Will Job or his friends dare to correct God?

Wisely, Job's answer is basically, "I'm going to shut up now" (40:3-5). God picks up His accusation again - "Who do you think you are?" Job confesses to God, "I have declared that which I did not understand, things too wonderful for me, which I did not know ... therefore I retract, and I repent in dust and ashes" (42:3, 6).

God accuses the three counselors of saying false things about Him to Job and tells them to ask Job to pray for them or they will be punished for the untrue things they have said about Job and about God. Job prays for them and God forgives them, and then He restores to Job double of everything that he had before the attack by Satan. The book ends with Job and his family enjoying all that God has given them, and Job dies an old man, "full of days" (Job 42:17).

To be honest, that ending really troubled me the first time I read Job. I was expecting God to give some awesome, all-explaining answer as to why good people suffer, why He let Satan attack Job, and why there is evil in the world. But He didn't. He just said in essence, "I am in charge. I know what I'm doing. And you couldn't possibly understand why I do what I do even if I tried to explain it to you" (Job 38 - 41). When I finally realized what God was doing in His answer, I was blown away! God asked Job for absolute trust in His goodness even though Job could never possibly understand why God does what He does, or doesn't do what He doesn't do. And that's the final answer to the theodicy question. We will never fully understand what God is doing (it is too much for us to comprehend), but we can still trust Him that what He's doing is good. The saying is surely true, "When you can't see His hand, trust His heart." This is a trust issue. You either trust Him, no matter what, or you don't.

Have you ever tried to explain to a two year old why he or she shouldn't eat certain things or do certain things or go certain places when the reasons for it were way beyond his or her understanding? You finally end up with that old parental standby: "Because I said so." Ultimately, obedience is a question of trust. It is impossible to explain everything to a two year old. Sometimes they just have to trust that you know what you are doing and that you are right ... whether you are a parent or God Himself.

LEARNING TO TRUST GOD

What does it mean to fully trust God? Well, at least three things: *(1) You accept everything that happens to you as something you are receiving from His hand.* Could God have prevented your accident, Joni's paralysis, your infection, your fall, your disease? Yes, of course He could have prevented it; but He didn't. Which means that He must have some purpose in allowing it in your life, because *(2) God knows what He's doing.* He is not surprised by what has happened to you. He has a good plan for your life - maybe not the most *comfortable* plan, but the *best* plan - and He is working out that plan through all the things that enter your life. Nothing ever touches your life without God's permission. Can I say that again: *nothing ever touches your life without God's permission!* He knows what He is doing with you, and He is working out His plan for your life ultimately to bring glory to Himself and to His kingdom and to bring others to salvation and spiritual maturity in Christ, because *(3) God is good and loving and He can be trusted.* His goodness does not always mean that He takes us down the easiest path, but it does mean

PRAISE GOD ... I'M SICK!

that He loves us and wants the very best for our lives so that they will count for eternity and bless others.

If you are confined to a bed right now, God has sent you there for a reason. He knows how to use your bedridden suffering for His purposes, and He is working out His plan in and through your life as you lie there. If you trust Him that much, He will show you what He has in mind for you and give you the power to do it for His glory! He may be calling you to strong, believing, prolonged prayer, or to counsel those who visit you, or to evangelize the medical professionals who take care of you, or to show unbelievers that Christians can have joy in spite of their circumstances in order to draw them to Jesus, or to teach your family members and friends the joy of serving someone less fortunate than they are, expecting nothing in return, or He may be doing some inner work in your heart that only suffering can accomplish.

I don't know what He has in mind, but I *know* that He has a loving plan for your life right where you are and that He can be trusted. As King David wrote, "Tremble [with anger or fear], and do not sin; meditate in your heart upon your bed, and be still. Offer the sacrifices of righteousness, and trust in the Lord" (Psalm 4:5). Like Job, we all must get to the point of not asking God *why* and start asking God *for what purpose in Your kingdom?* Then our sickbed can become a launching pad of blessing, and faith, and evangelism, and victory for us and for those around us.

That's the way it is with God. It's a trust issue. When we suffer, we are tempted to get angry with God, blame Him, complain against Him, doubt His love and wisdom, and even blame ourselves for not having enough faith or not being pure enough to get God to do what we want.

Sometimes we forget that we are dealing with the all-powerful Creator of the universe. He controls everything around us, has unlimited power, and has wisdom that we can't even begin to understand. It's a trust issue. Do you trust Him? If you do, you'll accept the easy *and* the hard from His hands, not asking "why," but asking "for what purpose, Lord?" How can I use this to bring glory and honor to my Lord? Job finally learned that when you don't understand everything, you can still trust the One who does! And that's the whole issue, isn't it?

3

MY ASSIGNMENT: THE SICK WITNESS

I wish I could tell you how many times I've been in the hospital, in doctors' offices, in labs, and in waiting rooms with nurses over the past few years. The employees in my pharmacy even greet me by name when I arrive at the drive-up window for a prescription, I have been there so often! If my bills are any indication, I have become one of the primary benefactors of the medical community in my city! I plan everything in my week around which doctors I am going to be visiting, on what day, and at what time.

THE SICK WITNESS

In the midst of all that mess, I have learned an important lesson. I have asked the Lord to make me His witness to all of those people. To start with, I ask Him to give me His joy as I go to the appointments. These poor people deal with depressed, downtrodden, bitter, angry victims of disease and suffering all day long. I have asked the Lord to help me provide a welcomed oasis from all of that for them. I joke with them, share the great things God is doing in my life, ask about their families, and I ask God to show me some way to encourage them and show them His love during every visit. There's a whole "mission field" out there of health professionals who desperately need to be encouraged and cared for as they care for us.

Hospital nurses are a prime target for me. You get to spend a great deal of time with them when you are hospitalized, and they can't really get away from you. Every time you buzz, they have to come, eventually! I have asked the Lord to make them want to come to my room because of my attitude of joy and my concern for them as people. A nurse told me recently during a six-hour blood transfusion that it was so much fun having me as a patient because it changed her whole day for the better. Who knew that blood transfusions could be fun!?!? That's the Lord!

Another nurse in an examination room responded to my usual, "And how are *you* doing?" with "Oh, OK." I knew something was wrong, so I asked the Lord to help me. I said that she seemed a little down. "Is something wrong?" I asked. "Yes, my mother died just a month ago and I can't seem to get over it." I asked her if her mom was a Christian and she said that she was a great Christian. Then I assured her that her mom was in Jesus' arms and was celebrating her new life with Him. Tears filled her eyes. "Will you be with her in heaven?" I asked. She assured me that she was a Christian, too, and that she knew that someday she would be with her mom in heaven, but she sure missed her here on earth. I asked, "Can I pray for you?" She nodded her head and walked over close to me. I put my hands on her shoulders and began to pray that the Lord would comfort her heart, assure her of her mom's home in heaven, and give her strength to live the life her mom would want her to live. As I prayed, tears streamed down her face. When I finished, she gave me a little hug, thanked me profusely, and went on to her next patient. That was the Lord!

That's my assignment. That's one of my "mission fields" - reaching out to nurses, doctors, surgeons, techs, receptionists, lab technicians, and other support staff with the Good News of the Gospel of Jesus Christ. Many of them spend most of their day dealing with people who are suffering; many are dying; and some have no hope at all. Their patients are sometimes angry, miserable, and combative. Many patients are easily irritated, and they sometimes take out their frustrations on the medical professionals trying to help them. These medical people need a break! And we can provide one for them by showing them the love of Christ.

THE DIFFERENCE JESUS MAKES IN OUR LIVES!

What a great opportunity this is to show the difference that Jesus makes in a person's life. Instead of anger, we show understanding and joy. Instead of self-centeredness, concern for *them*. Instead of bitterness, gratitude to God for our blessings. Instead of irritation, encouragement for the problems *they* are facing. Surely there is no greater contrast between the way a Christian acts and the way non-Christians act than what we do when we face suffering and death! We can reach out to those medical professionals and see our sickness as God's opportunity for us to touch their lives with the good news of the Gospel, lived out in us!

Recently I spoke with the surgical outpatient nurse who was caring for my wife. As we joked and chatted, God helped me insert a positive comment about how much knowing Him and worshipping Him with others in our church meant to us. She was interested in knowing more about our church, and guess what, two Sundays ago, she and her husband showed up for the service! Last Sunday they came back with two friends of theirs! Isn't God amazing? He can take the most unpleasant circumstances and use them for good in people's lives if we just let Him guide us and live through us!

PROVIDENTIAL ENCOUNTERS

I have learned to pray before I go in for an appointment that the Lord will open the door for me to witness to the staff and doctors. And He does it in miraculous ways. My cardiologist asked me one day, out of the blue, if I knew anything about "evidentialist apologetics." Now, I need to explain that the fact that he knew I was a college professor of religion made that question more understandable, but the circumstances were certainly God-ordered. He had been listening to the radio in his car and had come across a Christian station in which the speaker was explaining evidentialist apologetics, and it intrigued him, even though he is not a Christian. He had gone back to the station several times and really enjoyed the discussion. His question to me opened up a wonderful door of opportunity for witness that not only touched his life, but spilled over into the life of his assistant who came into the room to give me an EKG and overheard our discussion. That was the Lord! (By the way, in case you were wondering, *evidentialist apologetics* is the defense of the Christian faith based on substantial evidence that what it asserts is true).

My podiatrist, Dr. Scott Handley, and I have had so many discussions about the Lord and the Bible that some of his assistants vie for who gets to accompany him to care for me so they can listen in. One of them is now attending our church with her whole family. I show my interest in their lives and invite them to try Christ and His power to help them in their daily life situations. God has blessed those conversations, not only with the doctor, but with his staff as well. That is the Lord!

Recently, I went through another six-hour blood transfusion, this time with a man in the next bed who was dying of leukemia. I was able to share the Gospel with him and his wife, and they were thrilled to hear it. I guess I should definitely add that group in my assignment list - other sick people. The Lord has given me many wonderful opportunities to share the Gospel with people who are being treated for diseases like my own and who desperately need to hear a word of faith and hope from the Lord. The way the Lord puts me in the same room with those He has already started preparing for our conversation never ceases to amaze me. It's not a question of preaching a sermon or teaching a lesson - it's just sharing my own experience of the Lord's undergirding grace in my life in spite of my illnesses. God uses that simple testimony to touch people's hearts in spite of my stumbling attempts to witness. That is the Lord!

ACCEPTING GOD'S ASSIGNMENT

So, let me say this: those chances to touch people's lives would never have come to me if I weren't sick. Does that mean I *want* to be sick so that I can do that? Not really, but it does mean that I am thankful to the Lord that He can even use my sickness for good if I let Him. I have met literally dozens of nurses, doctors, techs, surgeons, and fellow patients that I would never have had contact with any other way. So, yes, I believe I am "on assignment." I am the "sick witness," called by God to take the Good News of Jesus Christ to that particular "mission field" of health professionals and patients to bring glory to His name. And if I have to be sick to do that, that's fine with me. I'd rather be well, but while I'm there anyway, I want God to use me to bless others. That's my assignment. That's the Lord!

4

SHOW THE WORLD!

The apostle Paul's life was a real mess. He seemed to go through life from crisis to crisis. When he lists his sufferings in 2 Corinthians 11, it seems almost impossible that one man could have gone through so much suffering in just one lifetime … especially a powerful servant of the Lord like Paul! He endured whippings of thirty-nine lashes (five times!); beatings with rods (three times!); stoning; shipwreck (three times!); dangers; hard labor; many sleepless nights; hunger; thirst; cold; exposure; and imprisonment (2 Corinthians 11:24-27). And on top of all that, he suffered from physical illness, too (2 Corinthians 12:7-10). What a life!

But Paul's reaction to all of that suffering was equally incredible: he wrote to the Colossians, "Now I *rejoice* in my sufferings for your sake" (Colossians 1:24). Was he out of his mind? No, he was Spirit-filled, God-called, God-sustained, and God's-purposes-driven! Paul was able to write, "Therefore we do not lose heart, but though our outer man is decaying, yet our inner man is being renewed day by day. For momentary, light affliction is producing for us an eternal weight of glory far beyond all comparison, while we look not at the things which are seen, but at the things which are not seen; for the things that are seen are temporary, but the things that are not seen are eternal" (2 Corinthians 4:16-18).

PAUL'S RESPONSE TO SUFFERING - IN DETAIL

The teaching in that passage is so crucial that it is worth a careful look as we face the reality of suffering in our lives today:

ONE: "*We do not lose heart*" - Paul had every reason in the world to lose heart, to be discouraged, and to want to give up, but he didn't. He was driven to carry out God's will for his life, no matter what it might cost him ... even his life.

TWO: *Our outer man is decaying, yet our inner man is being renewed day by day*" - This process of physical decay is exactly what this book is all about. Our physical self is decaying, falling apart; but our inner self, our spiritual self, is being renewed, restored, remade every day! *This has almost become my life verse!* Yes, my physical self is falling apart, but my spiritual self is being strengthened and fortified every day by the Lord! That's why Paul didn't lose heart ... because the most *important* part of his life was doing just fine, even if the physical part was decomposing every day. We must remember what is primary and what is secondary. Hard as it may be for some to believe, spirituality is primary; physicality is secondary. Paul had his priorities straight and he rejoiced in them.

THREE: "*For momentary, light affliction is producing for us an eternal weight of glory ... for the things that are seen are temporary, but the things which are not seen are eternal*" - In the light of eternity, Paul considered the terrible sufferings he was going through to be "momentary, light affliction." It is amazing to see what happens when we focus on eternity and get our eyes off our need for physical comfort, wellness, and ease. Paul had an eye for the eternal and the glory of heaven that was awaiting him, so the afflictions of this life seemed like nothing in comparison to that (see Romans 8:18). What are our minds set on - the eternal celebration of heaven or our temporary, earthly afflictions? As we concentrate on the glory awaiting us in eternity, the things of this world and the pain they produce grow dim in comparison. Sickness and suffering can have no power over a mind that is set on the coming glory of heaven!

A SPECIAL COMMISSION FROM THE LORD

Those of us who are going through sickness and suffering have a special commission from the Lord: show the world how a true Christian suffers. They may argue against our beliefs; they may make fun of our moral convictions; but they will sit back and take notice when we can do what they can never do - go through suffering with personal triumph and genuine joy. We are never in a better position to witness to the reality of the Gospel than when we are suffering. When we face sickness and death with faith, confidence, joy, and hope, the world stands with its mouth open and listens to our witness. Even in dealing with loved ones' deaths, as Paul wrote, we do "not grieve as do the rest who have no hope" (1 Thessalonians 4:13). The world is waiting for someone who can say, "All things work together for good," and really mean it.

MY MOTHER'S WITNESS IN DEATH

Some years ago, my mother became very sick. She was in her early sixties, and was diagnosed with incurable cancer. As my family visited her in the hospital, we joked and laughed and had a great time sharing with her and remembering crazy things that had happened to all of us. One day a rather perturbed nurse came into the room and asked me to come with her. She took me to a small room and said, "Do you people know how serious your mother's condition is?" I assured her that we were well aware that if the Lord didn't intervene miraculously, she would soon die. She responded, "Then, tell me, why are you all so happy?" I tried to explain to her that we would miss my mom if she died, but we were all absolutely sure that we would be with her again in heaven for all eternity, and that made us happy. She just shook her head and walked out.

My mother died soon after that. As I entered the pulpit to preach her funeral sermon, I noticed that very nurse sitting on the front row of the church. After the service, I thanked her for coming, espe-cially since she must have to deal with the deaths of so many cancer patients in her job. The nurse looked at me and said, "Many people have talked to me about giving my life to Christ, but I resisted all of them. But when I saw your mother going through such terrible pain with joy and hope and confidence of her home in heaven, I couldn't resist anymore. I gave my life to Christ."

SHOW THE WORLD

That's what I mean when I say, "Show the World!" They may not be swayed by our arguments or convinced by our rhetoric, but it is hard for the world to gainsay the witness of someone who has victory in the midst of pain, suffering, and even death. Maybe the Lord is calling you to that kind of witness. Maybe He longs to use your sickness right now to bless the lives of other people. Maybe they will never be more open to a testimony of the joy of knowing Jesus than when they see it come from your lips in spite of the hardship you are facing right now. Wouldn't it be glorious to meet someone in heaven who was there because your life of pain, joy, and hope won them over to faith in Christ? We need to show the world how a Christian suffers, and witness through our actions to the renewed, spiritual inner self in us that the Lord causes to grow stronger every day even as our outer self is decaying and falling apart! Show the world how a Christian suffers and God will use your joy and victory to bring them to Himself!

5

SPENDING MORE TIME WITH GOD THROUGH SICKNESS

We live in a world that is characterized by speed, by rushing, by the breakneck pace we set ourselves "to get everything done." Even Christians find themselves caught up in the rat race of over-commitment and frenetic activity. The opportunities to just sit back and think and pray and meditate are few and far between. Sickness and hardship, however, have a way of slowing us down. They make us put ourselves on the shelf for a while, and they give us time to think and spend time with the Lord.

PAUL'S TIME OUT
The apostle Paul was probably the most driven person in the Early Church. His work ethic was incredible. Not only did he travel and preach the Gospel, but he also paid his own way by working day and night at his tent-making business. Most of us would have fainted away with our tongues hanging out after just a month of the kind of schedule he kept. But God had something else planned for him. The Lord had something for Paul to do that required him to leave his extremely fruitful active ministry and spend long periods of time alone with God.

God wanted Paul to write almost half of the New Testament! So what did God do? He allowed two situations to sideline Paul from active ministry: imprisonment and sickness. Paul's sickness made him slow down his pace and spend time with God. And Paul's terms of imprisonment gave him time to write the Pauline prison epistles. While in prison, Paul wrote Ephesians, Colossians, Philippians, and Philemon. God turned around something that was patently unjust and cruelly punishing and made it into a blessing for Paul and all believers since that day. Isn't that just like the Lord?

MY TIME OUT, TOO

My life has seen the same kind of turnaround, but on a much smaller scale. I was privileged to teach world religions in a secular college for ten years after serving twenty years as a missionary in Colombia. More than seven thousand students passed through my classes during that decade. I was able to share the Gospel and my personal testimony with each of them! It was an ideal situation - something my wife and I had been praying to see happen for about twenty-five years. I could not have been happier in the place God had put me, and I worked hard to give my students the best presentations of the religions of the world I could possibly give. The Lord also allowed me to give my personal witness of salvation and walking with Jesus to every student who came through those classes.

About nine years ago, I began to have symptoms of heart trouble. Finally diagnosed as Congestive Heart Failure, the doctors did everything they could do to correct my heart, including stopping and restarting it, but it did not help much. I became weaker and weaker. I found it almost impossible to walk more than thirty or forty feet; I had trouble concentrating; I became dizzy when I stood up; and my ability to think on my feet became impaired. The college was very kind to me and gave me an office right across the hall from my lecture hall and even paid for a student assistant to help me in my duties, but my health continued to deteriorate. Finally, my cardiologist looked at me one day and said, "If you don't quit teaching, it's going to kill you. I don't know how you have been able to last this long."

I was heartbroken. I was not old enough to retire. The ideal situation into which God had placed me and the opportunity to reach thousands of college students with the Gospel began to evaporate before my eyes. I prayed and prayed, asking the Lord to heal me so that I could continue my ministry to them, but my health continued to decline. Many people cried out to God for me so that I could continue my ministry to those students, including some of my former students who had become Christians through the witness in my classes, but God chose not to answer those prayers with healing. I could not understand why, so I kept praying and praying.

One day as I was praying alone in my house, I asked the Lord if the reason I was not being healed was because He wanted me to quit teaching and do something else. In the deepest part of my soul, I heard Him say, "Yes." "Then what do you have for me to do, Lord?" I asked. The answer came back to my heart, "I want you to write." I struggled with that for a few seconds, then said, "OK, Lord, if that's what You want, I will do it."

That was almost eight years ago. In that time I have written two books, one of which has already been published (*Will the World End in 2012?*) and one, *Answers to Life's Toughest Questions,* which came out last year. This book will be the third one. I have already received news of people giving their lives to Christ as a result of the *2012* book, and many Christians used it to witness to their unbelieving friends, neighbors, and relatives. As of this date, over forty thousand copies have been sold in English, Spanish, Portuguese, and Polish. The *Answers to Life's Toughest* Questions book has helped many people deepen their faith and know how to answer others' questions. Whole Sunday School classes have ordered it from *Amazon.com* to use it as a study text. The Lord has graciously supported us financially so that vision could become a reality.

Is God good or what?!?! Would I ever have done that if I could have continued to teach? Absolutely not. I miss my students and faculty colleagues, but I picture those students in my mind every time I write and the faculty still invite me back for potluck suppers when they have one. He has used my sickness not only to turn me toward a new ministry, but He has also financed the writing ministry that He has called me to do. *God had a purpose in allowing me to be sick!* I have learned to trust Him even more through this experience and I challenge you to do the same. He knows what is best for me, and I trust Him to guide my life in the paths of greatest blessing for others. My one goal in life is to please Him and live for His glory, and I can do that sick or well.

MORE TIME WITH THE LORD

So, how does being sick sometimes bless us? Well, one of the ways is that it gives us more time to do things that we ordinarily would not have time to do. We can often spend long hours in prayer when we are sick, and catch up on all the people we promised, "I'll be praying for you." Because of our sickness, we can now make long lists of prayer requests and of people for whom to pray daily. And we can do it. My wife and I have met several bedridden saints who had maps of the world on their walls and spent many hours every day praying for each country in turn, that its people would be open to the Gospel and that missionaries there would be blessed in their ministries. Books like *The World Factbook* can be used as prayer guides. There are also many online prayer guidelines for the nations of the world that can help you focus your prayers on nation after nation like *PrayWay: Global Prayer Community*. Extended opportunities for prayer are a blessing when you are sick.

OUR WELSH EXAMPLE

Let me share about a lovely lady we met in Wales. She was very ill and could hardly get out of bed. She told us that many nights she could not sleep because of the pain she felt. So she turned on her radio to BBC World New s, and as they shared about some event in a given nation, she prayed for that country. She prayed that the missionaries there would be bring many people to faith in Christ. And she prayed that the national Christians would have a burning evangelistic zeal to reach their own people for Christ. She prayed that the unsaved of that country would hunger to know Jesus, be forgiven for their sins, and be born again. As she prayed on and on, she said, God would show her needs in the country and she would lift those needs to Him in prayer. She was a true inspiration to us, and we will never forget how the Lord used her, even in the midst of all of her sufferings. She taught us, by her example, many of the principles contained in this book.

WHEN WE'RE TOO SICK TO PRAY

Some people have told me that they were too sick even to pray. I understand that feeling, but it doesn't have to stop you. You can ask God to bring people's faces to your mind and just silently ask the Lord to bless them as you see them. And let's remember God's great promise in Romans 8:26-27. Sometimes we are too weak even to know what to pray, but the Holy Spirit helps us, as He "intercedes for us with groanings too deep for words." He knows our hearts and He intercedes "according to the will of God." What a great promise! When we get so weak that we can't even pray, the Holy Spirit takes over for us and prays through us according to God's will, and great things happen!

EXTRA TIME IN GOD'S WORD

Times of sickness can be times of blessing when we can also spend long periods of time studying God's Word. Get a good exhaustive concordance. Look up all the uses of words like faith, love, holy, mercy, grace or hope. Make a list of all the biblical passages that use the word, then look at each passage to summarize on your sheet what it teaches about that word. Finally, organize what you have found using categories like: origin, results, means, definition, expression of, contrasts, related terms, etc. It will take hours and hours to do that kind of study of words that are used a great deal in Scripture, but you will be amazed at how your understanding of God's Word and the Christian life grows as you study. If you have plenty of time on your hands, use it well!

TIME TO TALK ABOUT THE LORD

God can also use your sickness to give you time to talk to people about Him. How about focusing on your children or grandchildren, spending quality time with each of them and talking to each one of them in depth about their faith in the Lord and their walk with Him? You can also spend time sharing your faith with those who visit you "on your bed of affliction." Your testimony of joy in spite of trials may well inspire them to take a new look at their circumstances and give thanks to God for what they have and the quality of their lives.

THE "ROYAL PRIESTHOOD" INCLUDES ALL OF US!

You may be struggling right now with why God has "put you on the shelf." You may not be able to see any purpose in the suffering you are going through. You may feel dejected, depressed, and useless, but *God has a purpose for your life!* He uses every one of His children to bless others, and you are no exception to that promise. He has ordained you to be part of "a royal priesthood, a holy nation, a people for God's own possession, so that *you* may proclaim the excellencies of Him who has called you out of darkness into His marvelous light ... for you have been called for this *purpose*, since Christ also suffered for you, leaving you an example for you to follow in His steps ... while suffering, He [Jesus] uttered no threats, but kept *entrusting* Himself to Him who judges righteously" (1 Peter 2:9, 21, 23). Jesus is the perfect example of trusting God in the midst of suffering, and He calls us to "follow in His steps."

There *is* purpose in your life as you trust in God and offer your suffering to Him in obedience to His calling on your life. Like every other Christian, you are *called by God* to "proclaim His excellencies" to those around you. And how better could you do that than to show them that you are trusting God in your suffering and believing Him to work out His purposes in and through your life and use you to bless others? The extra time you have to spend with the Lord because of your illness will give you even more opportunities to tune in to exactly what He has for you to do! He has called you apart from your normal activities for a reason: to be with Him and serve Him in prayer, Bible study, and testimony. Don't miss this great opportunity to spend more time with God through sickness!

6

CONSIDER IT ALL JOY, ANYWAY!

Every Monday night, all the missionaries in our group in Colombia met together for a prayer meeting. Each of us was asked to share something from God's Word in turn. As a brand new missionary, it was my night to share and I chose James 1:2-4 as my text. I tried to lay out the logic of the passage:

CONSIDER IT ALL JOY WHEN YOU ENCOUNTER VARIOUS TRIALS:

But how can we do that? It doesn't seem logical. Trials do *not* produce joy! But the rest of the passage reveals the secret: how can we consider it to be joy when we encounter trials?

First, by "knowing that the testing of your faith produces endurance."

Second, by letting "endurance have its perfect result, so that you may be perfect and complete, lacking in nothing." So, the formula is:

A. The testing of your faith produces endurance.
B. Endurance produces a Christian who is perfect, complete, lacking in nothing (*prepared for anything!*)
C. Therefore: consider it all *joy* when you encounter trials because:

Testing -> Endurance -> Prepared for anything -> Joy!

I began to bring the lesson of the passage home: everyone wants to be perfect (*teleios,* in Greek = capable of carrying out the function for which you were created - "purpose-ready"), and complete (*holokleiros* = sound, whole, complete), lacking in nothing (*leipo* = falling short/lacking in nothing). That is the ideal Christian life: ready for what God wants us to do with all we need to do it! But how do we attain it? Well, according to James, it is through trials! Trials, which test your faith, produce *endurance* (*hupomonei* = patient endurance, steadfastness, perseverance), and *endurance* will make us *teleios, holokleiros,* and *en meideni leipomenoi*: purpose-ready, complete, and lacking in nothing. (I knew just enough Greek then to be dangerous!)

So, trials test our faith. They tempt us not to have faith … not to believe that God loves us, wants the best for us, or cares about us. Trials depress us. They discourage us. They sadden us. *But,* says James, we should "consider it all joy" when we have to face trials because they have a great purpose in our lives. As the trial tests our faith (and we pass the test!), we learn *patient endurance, steadfastness, and perseverance*! And those character traits make us "purpose-ready" and "complete, lacking in nothing." You see, if we can endure trials with joy, what can possibly get to us? Who can destroy our faith? What suffering can take away our confidence in the Lord? What can possibly shake us? As a preacher once said, "God is more interested in the production of character than in the provision of comfort." And it is *character* that makes us ready for *anything*!

As I finished my presentation to the missionaries, one of the ladies said, "That's ridiculous! How can you consider something bad to be a joy? That's crazy!" Well, that started a discussion among the missionaries present that went on for quite a while. We almost forgot to have our snacks!

Some insisted, "If that's what the Bible says, then that's what we are supposed to do." Others said, "Yes, but it can't possibly mean that. It must mean something else." As they argued back and forth, I stayed in the background and listened to them. I was a brand new missionary, my first year there, and I was just getting to know all of them. But as they talked, I began to see that there were two groups among them: the "God-knows-what-He's-doing-and-I-trust-Him" group and the "I-don't-know-how-many-more-trials-I-can-take" group.

As we lived and ministered among them for the next twenty years, it became more and more apparent that some were joyous, confident, and victorious while others were defeated, worn out, and discouraged. My wife and I decided right there which group we wanted to join, and we have found that God is always willing to help us "consider it all joy" if we ask Him to do it. Not that we did it perfectly all the time, but that was our goal in every trial that we had to go through, and God kept His promise when we put our faith in Him.

TRIALS IN COLOMBIA

During those years in Colombia, we went through many testings of our faith. We struggled with sicknesses, danger, an attempted kidnapping of one of our kids, a poisonous snake in our living room, threats to kill me by Marxist guerrillas, a near-attack by a huge black panther, rejection and hostility from some Colombians, the murder of one of our missionaries, stoning of Sharyn when she was eight months pregnant, lack of water, lack of electricity, constant killings in our neighborhood, grueling trips into the jungle, the bombing of the house across the street from us, near death in a river whirlpool, chronic overwork, fatigue, a machine gun fight on our street, many bouts of sickness for all of us, and many other trials. But God helped us, and I can say that in spite of all of those difficulties we had to face, God was teaching us to experience a supernatural joy that Satan could not take away, though he tried very hard. God can help totally ordinary people live in victory when they depend on Him!

"IN-SPITE-OF" JOY

I know of many missionaries who have experienced the same thing. Late at night, sitting in the dark, they have cried out to God with what seemed to be their last ounce of strength, and He has come to them and given them a joy that this world knows nothing about. It is the kind of "in-spite-of" joy that rises above the circumstances of life and spiritually "intoxicates" the spirit of a person with assurance and hope and confidence in the Lord and His great power and awesome wisdom. And as they endure the trial, a spiritual steel begins to take shape in their soul that nothing and no one can break or even bend. It becomes a spiritual backbone that gets them through the hard times, not just barely, but victoriously.

CONSIDER IT ALL JOY!

I don't know what you are going through right now, but I'm sure you have trials of your own. I want to echo the words of James, "Consider it all joy!" God is at work through those trials, testing your faith and producing patient endurance in you that nothing can shake, equipping you to do what God has called you to do for His glory. You can then thank Him for the supernatural joy He gives you when everything around you is trying to drag you down into defeat, discouragement, and depression. Once God does that for you - gives you that kind of joy in the face of trials - your life will never be the same! So, count it all joy and give God the glory for your "in-spite-of-no-matter-what-happens" faith, joy, and trust in Him.

7

HOW TO BECOME GRUMBLE-PROOFED

I'm sure that one of the biggest temptations those of us who suffer with illnesses for a long time experience is the temptation to *grumble*. We grumble to our friends and our relatives: "I just don't know why the Lord doesn't heal me. You know, that Susan was healed last month and she's not half the Christian I am. I wish the Lord would answer my prayers. Sometimes I feel like God doesn't listen to me anymore. I don't think I can stand much more of this without either losing my mind or losing my faith, or both!"

OUR GRUMBLING AND OTHERS

Maybe unbelievers in restaurants and doctors' offices overhear us grumbling and think, "He's so miserable and complaining. And he's supposed to be a Christian!" Our friends and relatives sigh when they see us coming because they know they are about to hear the latest edition of the "Disastergram." We often share every ache, every pain, every discomfort, every new symptom, and every possible new disease with such excruciating detail that people tire of hearing us talk. And what about our doctors?!? They are forced to listen on and on as some patients regale them with every twinge and every discomfort, grumble upon grumble. Grumbling can almost become an addiction for those of us who suffer ill health. We become addictive sympathy-seekers, looking for that soothing, "Oh, you poor thing. I don't know how you stand it. You're so brave to put up with all that. It's just not right that so many bad things happen to you." That's what they *say* to us, but on the inside, they are often thinking, "Oh, give me a break!"

GOD'S VIEW OF GRUMBLING

But wait a minute. Don't we have a right to grumble? I mean, it *does hurt*. It *is* painful. It *is* difficult to put up with it. *We* deserve better. Or do we? The Bible paints a very clear picture of what God thinks about grumbling ... He hates it! It angers Him. He judges it to be a lack of faith and trust in Him. And He punishes it. Grumbling is one of the things that God can't stand. It accomplishes nothing positive. It robs us of our faith in Him. It makes us doubt His goodness. It reveals an arrogant "I-deserve-better" spirit that expresses itself in self-centered complaints and protests. Grumbling is a bitter outward projection of an inward egotistical mindset. It is antithetical to the kind of grateful, trusting, self-effacing, submissive spirit that Christians are supposed to exemplify.

THE PEOPLE OF ISRAEL - CHAMPION GRUMBLERS

The people of Israel had a dismal record of grumbling against their leaders and against God Himself. Two weeks after leaving Egypt and its slavery and death, the Israelites wandered in the desert and were hungry. They began to complain against Moses and Aaron for bringing them out of Egypt "to kill this whole assembly with hunger" (Exodus 16:3). Moses wisely told them that they were not grumbling against him, but against the Lord: "... you will see the glory of the Lord [when He supplies manna in the morning and meat in the evening], for He hears your grumblings against the Lord; and what are we that you grumble against us?" (Exodus 16:7). God abundantly supplied them with food, and they went on their way.

But soon after, they traveled to Rephidim and began grumbling to Moses that there was no water to drink. They again accused Moses of bringing them out of Egypt only to kill them in the desert with thirst (Exodus 17:1-3). Once again, Moses wisely turned to God. The Lord told him to strike a rock with his staff and water gushed out of it for the people to drink. But Moses called the place "Massah and Meribah." In Hebrew, *Massah* means test and *Meribah* means quarrel "because of the quarrel of the sons of Israel, and because they tested the Lord, saying, 'Is the Lord among us, or not?" (Exodus 17:6-7). Like many of us, their suffering made them wonder if God had abandoned them. Their grumbling was an expression of their lack of faith and trust in the Lord. They were looking for instant results to meet their every need, but God was using delayed gratification to test them to see if they would trust Him. Once again, their grumbling made them fail the test, but God was gracious and merciful to them anyway.

GRUMBLING AGAINST MOSES
The book of Numbers records several grumbling episodes against Moses and against God Himself (chapters 14, 16, and 17). They grumbled about the Promised Land and its large inhabitants, and God said that none of them would enter that land alive (Numbers 14). They grumbled about the leadership of Moses and Aaron, and more than 14,000 died by plague (Numbers 16). The initial result of their grumbling was that God sent them in circles in the desert for forty years. Actually, it took them forty years to make a two-week trip, until the Lord declared, "You have circled this mountain long enough. Now turn north" (Deuteronomy 2:3).

The final result of their grumbling was that God concluded that they had put Him to the test ten times; they had not listened to His voice; they believed He hated them and had brought them into Canaan to be killed; they rebelled against Him; and they did not trust Him (Numbers 14 and Deuteronomy 1). So, He decided that none of the people of that generation would ever enter Canaan - they would all die in the desert - and their children would inherit the land He had promised to give them (Numbers 14, Deuteronomy 1). That was the penalty for grumbling - not because of the act in itself, but for what it demonstrated about their rebellion, distrust, and refusal to obey God. Their grumbling cost them everything. God judged them for the attitude that many still have today: if He doesn't do what I want when I want, then He's no God of mine!

PAUL ON GRUMBLING

The apostle Paul reminds us that as Christians, we need to be very careful not to "grumble, as some of them [the Israelites] did, and were destroyed by the destroyer. Now these things happened to them as an example, and they were written for our instruction" (1 Corinthians 10:10-11). Grumbling is a sin for Christians just as it was for the Israelites, and we need to avoid it at all cost.

GRUMBLING VERSUS TRUSTING GOD

Why do we grumble? It is, again, a trust issue. If we believe that God is guiding our lives and that His will is always good for accomplishing His purposes through us and that He knows what He's doing, we won't grumble when hard times come our way. We will accept what comes from His hand and believe that He will either solve the problem or use it for His glory. Grumbling short-circuits the process.

God has two ways of bringing glory to His Name and to His Kingdom when we suffer. He can heal us and show His mighty power and His loving mercy, or He can walk with us through the suffering, giving us joy and hope and trust in the midst of it and show the depth of His powerful transformation of our lives. The important issue is that it is God, not we, who makes the choice of which way to glorify His Name and His Kingdom when we suffer.

I call the two ways the "Hallelujah Road" and the "Hallelujah-in-spite-of-it Road." I'm sure we would all prefer the first road. It's easier, more comfortable, less stressful and painful. But when you see the results of the two roads, it becomes more difficult to say which one you may prefer. If my "unhealed" illness can bring people to salvation in Christ, give me extra time with the Lord, enable me to do things I wouldn't have time to do otherwise, encourage my friends and relatives to trust God more and rejoice in their trials, and minister to God's heart when He knows I suffer and still trust and love Him, doesn't that make the "Hallelujah-in-spite-of-it Road" seem a good bit more appealing? In the final analysis, it is a question of what kind of trust we have in God.

THE THREE LEVELS OF TRUST
There are three basic levels of trust in God: baby trust, teenage trust, and mature trust. Each level has its own characteristics:

Baby Trust: these people trust God as long as He does exactly what they want. He has to supply their needs, solve their problems, and answer their prayers with "yes" or they throw a spiritual tantrum. Grumbling and demanding that God do *their* will are two of their favorite pastimes.

Teenage Trust: These people trust God, but only if they can understand what He is doing. They want to know why He does or doesn't do something, and they are not content until they get answers. They refuse to accept the "because I said so" answer to their questions, and they trust God only as far as they can see a good reason to do so. Grumbling is one of their favorite hobbies because they often don't understand what God is doing and they complain about that to their seemingly attentive friends.

Mature Trust: these people trust God no matter what happens. They believe that nothing can touch their lives without God's permission and they are willing to wait patiently to see how God wants to use a difficult situation to bring glory to His Name and to His Kingdom. When they suffer, they don't ask "why," they ask "for what purpose, Lord?" They count it all joy when they have trials because they know that trials are God's way of developing patient endurance in them and making them mature and complete for everything God wants to do in and through their lives. They don't grumble; they pray and trust. When they suffer, their faith and trust bring praise to God and draw other people to faith in Him.

BECOMING GRUMBLE-PROOF

So, how can we become "grumble-proof" as Christians? Very simply … *trust God.* Totally surrender your life to Him, trusting that He knows what's best for you and that He is working out His eternal purposes in everything that happens to you … both the pleasant things and the hard ones. Realize that you live in a fallen world where suffering, pain, and disappointment come to us all. Accept your present circumstances as a calling from the Lord to bring glory to His Name in a unique way that will bring unbelievers to faith in Him and challenge believers to greater trust, hope, and victory in spite of trials. As your faith, trust, and hope grow, you will find God giving you more and more opportunities to show His mighty power in and through your life. His power is made perfect in our weakness! There is no room for grumbling in a life of absolute trust and surrender to God. And that's how we become "grumble-proofed!"

8

WHY ME, LORD?

I want to make it clear that what I have said above is in no way meant to trivialize the suffering that people endure. My father-in-law died of throat cancer at the age of forty. His last months of life were filled with terrible suffering, pain, and helplessness. My wife's uncle died of emphysema. His last months were dominated by relentless suffocation as his lungs continually filled up with fluid, making it almost impossible for him to breathe. Many of my friends and relatives have ended their lives in unspeakable torment and anguish. We never want to give the impression as Christians that we minimize the horror of those ghastly experiences. Still, in the midst of all that agony, we want to affirm that God's Word is true, God's power is greater than our suffering, and God's grace can enable us to get through even the most horrifyingly devastating situations with victory, hope, and even joy.

WHY ME?

It is also true that when many sincere Christians encounter hardships and affliction, the question that leaps out of their hearts is, "Lord, why me?" It is almost impossible not to ask that question in your heart even if you never vocalize it out loud. Why would God allow such a thing to happen to me? What have I done to deserve this?

Why won't God answer my prayers and deliver me out of this? Why can't I move the hand of God? Why me???

There are many possible answers to that question. Let's consider some of them:

A. Why not us? Maybe the Lord is trying to teach us that our faith is no guarantee of a problem-free life. As C. S. Lewis put it, "The real problem is not why some pious, believing people suffer, but why some do not." Regardless of how godly our lives are, we are not immune from the sufferings of this world. So many Christians have been infected, consciously or unconsciously, by the germ of Radical Prosperity Theology and have come to believe that their faith is a shield against suffering. They hold the unhealthy view that being a Christian means healing from all diseases and deliverance from all problems. That is simply not true. If we harbor those erroneous thoughts in our mind, allowing suffering to enter our lives may be God's most effective antidote to that infection. So maybe that's why we are going through this ... for our own ultimate good and correction.

B. Maybe the Lord wants to produce patient endurance in us. There is only one sure path to patience and endurance, and it is the path of trials. God sometimes allows suffering in our lives to develop the character we need for some great purpose He has for our lives. If that is what God is doing, we can genuinely consider this trial to be a *joy* because we know that God is using it to prepare us for greater things in the future.

C. Maybe the Lord allows it so that we can have more time to spend with Him or to accomplish something He wants us to do. God does sometimes "put us on the shelf" in order to have more time of loving fellowship and faith-filled prayer with us. There may be something God wants us to do that we will never get to if we continue our usual activities, so He sets us aside for a while to give us time to do that. In either case, this time of diminished activity is intended for our good and for the advancement of God's plans for our lives. We should accept it from His hand and spend time with Him in prayer to see how He would have us use it for His glory.

D. Maybe the Lord allows it to test the level of our trust in Him. It's easy to trust God when everything is going great, but when things begin to fall apart and our world begins to crumble around us, that is when we find out how deeply we trust in Him and believe He works all things "for good." Maybe the Lord is now trusting you with a deeper level of faith - faith that is like bedrock - unshakable, strong, and unmovable. That iron-strong faith can stand up to anything that comes, and it is worth whatever it takes to get it. It will change our lives and give us something to fall back on, no matter what happens in the future.

E. Maybe the Lord is calling us to be "sick witnesses." The world is hungry for genuine Christians who can endure sickness and pain with joy and hope and overcoming faith. God may well want to use us to bring our nurses, doctors, technicians, and fellow patients to faith in Him. What a privilege!

F. Maybe the Lord allows it to show us (and those around us) that the power in our life and ministry is in Him, not in us. The apostle Paul learned this lesson through his own sufferings. They kept him humble and focused on God's ability, not his own. Paul believed that his physical weaknesses and repellent appearance made it easier for people to attribute his powerful ministry to God, not to himself. God may also be using our sickness to drive that lesson home, both to us and to those around us, so that we can enjoy an amazing ministry that brings glory to Him, not to ourselves.

G. Maybe the Lord wants to use our weakness to teach our relatives and friends the grace of caring for the sick. Those of us who have spent our lives caring for others find it especially difficult to accept the care of others for us. I have had to counsel some older saints to quit refusing help and gracefully accept the attention and care of others when they can no longer care for themselves. Our ability to do that can be used by God to prepare our friends and relatives for that day in their own lives. God may also use our needs to soften their hearts and help them not to be so self-centered and self-absorbed. Showing love to someone who cannot do anything to repay you is good for the soul.

H. Maybe God allows it in order to use our lives and our sufferings to show people the joy that a Christian can have, even in the face of serious adversity. When we are in pain, when our life force is ebbing away, when we are helpless and dependent on others, the natural response is anger, fear, and bitterness. The fact that Christians can show remarkable joy and selfless love in the middle of all of that is one of the greatest testimonies to the existence, the power, and the presence of God that we can ever give. God may well be calling us to a golden moment of witness through these sufferings so that the world can know that He lives and that He can transform lives!

I. Maybe the Lord wants us to accept this from His hand with faith, trust, love, and hope, without ever knowing why He has allowed it. That was the lesson Job learned. Ultimately, it is a matter of trust. We may never know why we have to go through the suffering we experience, but we can still trust God that He knows what He is doing and that His plan for our lives is perfect. Joni Eareckson Tada has recently written a new book entitled *A Place of Healing: Wrestling with the Mysteries of Suffering, Pain, and God's Sovereignty.* In it, she admits that she does not fully understand why God allowed her to become paralyzed or why He has allowed her to contract breast cancer. But she does know that He is sovereign, that His will is good, and that the things He allows in her life are for the furtherance of the Gospel. We must all eventually come to that place of faith and trust in Him.

Suffering can be used by God to fast track us to that destination, for His glory.

J. Maybe the Lord is calling us to Himself through this sickness to usher us into His presence in heaven. God does not see death and entering heaven as a tragedy in our lives. Sooner or later, we all walk through that door. The question is not, "Will I die?" but rather, "How well will I die?" Will I die with words of hope and faith and joy on my lips or screams of panic and terror? God may be calling us to Himself through our illness, and if He is, praise His name! One step into heaven will erase all fear and concern from our hearts and cause us to explode with a celebration of praise for all God has prepared for us! If God is calling you to Himself, get ready for the most exciting, amazing, astonishing event in your life! You are going to see the King, and be wrapped up in His arms of love. As you enter heaven, He will say, "Well done, good and faithful servant ... enter into the *joy* of your master" (Matthew 25:21). You have made it! You are on the doorstep of eternity! God holds out His arms, welcoming you to your eternal home! If God calls you, step through that door with faith and confidence and victory and joy. You are going home! Praise Him!

Whatever God has in mind through the illnesses we endure, the one constant is that He wants to use our lives for His glory and to advance His Kingdom through us regardless of the situations we are facing. He has promised to go with us through every experience of life and bring us through them, not just "by the skin of our teeth," but victoriously! As Paul writes, "in all these things we overwhelmingly conquer through Him who loved us" (Romans 8:37). Illness is no exception to that promise. If we seek His will in our suffering, pray for His strength, and trust in His goodness, we are inviting Him to bring good out of bad circumstances and victory out of intended defeat. How it must warm the heart of God when we trust Him in and through our illnesses to bring blessing to others in spite of our difficulties and challenges!

> *May God bless each of us who suffer without being healed (at least, not yet) so that we can be a real blessing to all around us and live for the praise of His glory!*

TO SUM IT UP ...

Let me say this to balance things out a bit: seek to be healed! Pray for your own healing. Ask people to pray that you be healed. Do everything your doctors say you should do to improve your health. Spend long periods of time in fasting (if you can) and prayer, seeking the Lord and His healing power. Believe God that He is Healer and that He is more than powerful enough to heal you of any disease or sickness. Trust Him to heal you, and unite in prayer with others for your healing. But if He chooses not to heal you, know that this experience is not a detour in your life, but an opportunity for Him to do things in and through you that could never happen otherwise.

I don't wish sickness and suffering on anyone - not even on the guy who rear-ended me last week - but I know that sooner or later we will all go down that path. Our bodies are not meant to be eternal, and they break down and wear out, whether we like it or not. My main concern is that we not see times of sickness as a parenthesis in our lives, but rather, as an opportunity for blessing.

My prayer is that this book has demonstrated some of the ways that God can use sickness to bless your life and the lives of those around you. Sickness is not a detour from God's plan for us; it's just another path we have to follow for a while. And it's a path God can use to bless us and others if we let Him. There are lessons to be learned, witness opportunities to take, and new levels of trust in God to be attained. And it all comes through sickness and suffering. Far from being a detour away from our "real life," illness is an opportunity to see God work truths and traits into our lives that don't come any other way. As a radio Bible teacher once said, "Anything that makes me need God more in my life is a blessing!" I believe that. Do you?

Too many people take their time of illness as an interruption in their service for God. They put their lives on hold and "wait until it's over." But that's not how God sees it. God sees times of sickness, suffering, and trials as opportunities to do "a new thing" in our lives that will result in a deeper walk with Him and the blessings that He can only give us when we are weak and He is strong.

Not only can those times be a time of blessing for us, but they can be a time of blessing *through us* to others. God can use our suffering to inspire others to believe in Him and His ability to turn even difficult situations into victories of His grace and power. As we go through illnesses with joy and hope and confidence in Him, God can use our surprising witness to His goodness to convince others that it is worthwhile to trust Him as well. The world is waiting on tiptoes to see if Christians can really go through crushing circumstances with supernatural joy and the bedrock assurance that He is in control and that He can use anything that comes to us to bring praise to His mercy, His grace, and His amazing power. You may never have a better opportunity to witness to your faith in Christ than when you are suffering. Non-believers will listen to someone who can pass through the trials of life with a cheerfulness and a contentment that they could never manufacture in a million years on their own. Of course, we can't either, but we have Someone living in us and with us who can do the impossible through us!

One last thought: someday we will all face that ultimate suffering, death. We will either face it with confidence and victory or we will face it with horror and fear. Our extended family members will never forget how we died. It is our last chance to show them how a Christian lives and how a Christian dies.

In the basement of the church that John Wesley founded in Bristol, England, there are plaques that cover the walls that are dedicated to Wesley's early preachers. Surprisingly, the texts on them do not describe their ministries or their walk with the Lord; they describe their deaths. Each one tells how that preacher passed into eternity, quoting his last words and demonstrating the depth of his faith in Christ and his confident joy as he slipped into heaven. Apparently, the early Methodists were convinced that the way a person dies puts the exclamation point on how they lived. That is still true today.

Make it a good death! Walk into heaven with praise on your lips and God's joy in your heart. Make your family gasp with amazement at how your face lights up as you see Jesus coming for you. You have every reason to be ecstatically happy. The diseases that ravage your body do not win ultimately - you do! Long after those cancerous tumors have starved and died in a Christian's buried body, that Christian will be more alive than ever before! You will be enjoying more delight; you will be seeing more beauty; you will be hearing greater singing; and you will be basking in the light of the glory of Jesus Christ, God the Father, and the Holy Spirit. Christians, be happy ... WE WIN! And God will wipe away every tear from our eyes and give us "joy unspeakable and full of glory" in His presence, forever and ever!

Dr. Raymond C. Hundley, a retired college professor of World Religions, received his religious education in Asbury Theological Seminary in Lexington, the University of Cambridge in England, and Trinity Evangelical Divinity School in Chicago. Dr. Hundley holds the Master of Arts in Religion degree in biblical literature, the Master of Letters degree in theology, and the Ph.D. in systematic theology, respectively. He and his wife were missionaries in Colombia, South America, for twenty years. He has given conferences on religious topics in Europe, Asia, Africa, Latin America, and North America, and was a consultant for the World Evangelical Alliance when it met in Singapore in 1986. He has also served as a youth evangelist, pastor, professor, and mission director. He is a published author, having written three books and more than thirty articles and book chapters. He was professor of hermeneutics and academic dean of the Seminario Bíblico de Colombia for two decades, and is currently a visiting adjunct professor at the European Nazarene College in Büsingen, Switzerland, and has taught pastoral studies in the U.S., Costa Rica, Russia, and Ukraine. He and his wife, Sharyn, live in Sarasota, Florida, where he teaches a large Sunday School class for adults.

41383369R00040

Made in the USA
Charleston, SC
29 April 2015